STRIDERS

The Great Bok Gathering

SCHOLASTIC

Published in the UK by Scholastic Education, 2024
Scholastic Distribution Centre, Bosworth Avenue,
Tournament Fields, Warwick, CV34 6UQ
Scholastic Ireland, 89E Lagan Road, Dublin Industrial
Estate, Glasnevin, Dublin, D11 HP5F

www.scholastic.co.uk
© 2024 Scholastic
1 2 3 4 5 6 7 8 9   4 5 6 7 8 9 0 1 2 3

Printed by Ashford Colour Press

The book is made of materials from well-managed,
FSC®-certified forests and other controlled sources.

A CIP catalogue record for this book is available from the
British Library.

ISBN 978-0702-32734-6

Author
Giles Clare

Editorial team
Rachel Morgan, Vicki Yates, Sasha Morton,
Jennie Clifford

Design team
Dipa Mistry, Andrea Lewis and We Are Grace

Photograph
p4 (background) vectopicta/Shutterstock

Illustrations
Berat Pekmezci/The Bright Agency

How to use this book

This book practises these letters and letter sounds:

ey (as in 'they')	kn (as in 'knock')	su (as in 'measured')
si (as in 'television')	ge (as in 'strange')	y (as in 'mystery')
ti (as in 'protection')	ci (as in 'delicious')	ore (as in 'before')

Here are some of the words in the book that use the sounds above:

usually confusion more large special know

This book uses these common tricky words:

thought were today aren't the of said once do to their are people because whole beautiful into one sure

About the series

This is the fourth book in a series about a boy called Nick who finds an unusual bug and takes it home to look after it. In previous books Bok escapes several times and Nick and his family begin to question whether it's right to keep him as a pet.

Before reading

- Read the title and look at the cover. Discuss what the book might be about.
- Talk about the characters on page 4 and read their names.
- The story is split into chapters shown by numbers at the top of the page.

During reading

- If necessary, sound out and then blend the sounds to read the word: g-a-th-er-i-ng, gathering.
- Pause to talk about the story.

After reading

- Talk about what you have read.

1

Bok usually thought bananas and syrup were delicious, but today he had lost his appetite. "Hey, buddy, why aren't you hungry this morning?" asked Nick.

Just then, a scream came from the lounge.
"It's Bok! Quick, come and see!" cried Nan.

Mum and Nick looked at each other in confusion.

They found Nan pointing at the television.
"What's the matter, Nan?" asked Nick.
"There's more of them in the forest.
Your precious Bok is part of an invasion.
Look!" said Nan.

Nick gasped in surprise. The news report was showing pictures of Bok. In fact, it was showing thousands of creatures just like Bok.

An insect specialist called Dylan appeared on screen.

"These strange insects typically only emerge from underground once every eight years," he explained.

"They sprout wings and gather in large colonies in the forest, where they put on an amazing dance display. Why they do this is a mystery, but it seems to be a special stage in their life cycle."

TV6

"I knew it! They're taking over," cried Nan. "It's a huge gang of Boks."

"We're keeping their location a secret for their protection," added Dylan. "We know these creatures are unusual, but we urge people not to interfere with them."

"Poor Bok," said Nick. "I thought looking after him was the right decision. What should we do now?"

2

The next day, there was a knock at the door.
"Hi. Thanks for calling me," said Dylan, the
insect specialist. "Where is the little dude?"
"I call him Bok," said Nick.

Dylan examined Bok and measured him.
"Well, Bok is still in great condition, but
he will be more cheerful once he returns
to his colony," said Dylan.

"Please can we come with you to release Bok?" asked Nick.
"Hmm, I don't usually give permission for that, but I can make an exception because you have looked after Bok so well," replied Dylan.

He put Bok inside a box, and they all set off to take him home.

3

An astonishing sight waited in the forest.
The whole forest floor was covered with
dancing insects.

"It's time," said Dylan.
Nick knelt down and opened the box.
"So long, buddy. I'll miss you," he said.

Bok edged out of the box. His beautiful blue wings shimmered in the sunlight. Mum took a final photo.

"Bok Bok, Nick," said Bok.

"Hey, did you just...?" said Nick. Before he could finish, Bok took off to explore.

At the same moment, there was an explosion of sound. A huge cloud of insects surged into the air. Bok flew straight over to join them.

"Where are they going?" asked Mum.
"No one knows for sure," replied Dylan.
"Magical, isn't it?"

Back at home, Mum and Nick agreed it had been a special but sad occasion. Nan was looking at the photo Mum had taken.
"I thought you would be pleased," Mum said to Nan.
"I miss Bok!" she croaked.